HAVE SALE - WILL TRAVEL

$ecrets of an Estate-$ale Agent

★ A Users Guide To The Perfect Estate Sale ★

Betty DeKlyne

Illustrations by
Craig Bonner

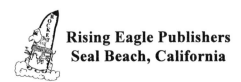

Rising Eagle Publishers
Seal Beach, California

Have Sale - Will Travel
Secrets of an Estate-Sale Agent

Copyright © 1996 by Betty DeKlyne
Second Printing 1997

For information, address Rising Eagle Publishers,
P.O. Box 3813, Seal Beach California, 90740-7813

First Edition
Library of Congress Catalog Card Number 96-92049
ISBN 0-9651559-0-0

Printed by Spinelli Graphics

Rising Eagle logo is a Trademark of Rising Eagle Publishers

ACKNOWLEDGMENTS

I'd like to thank the following people for their help in making this book possible.

Lowell & Dorothy Johnson - who taught me the business; Leslie Juchna - for all her hours and hours of secretarial work and editing; Bill Shelton - for his encouragement and extensive copy-editing based on his many years of newspaper experience; all my friendly readers and encouragers - Patricia Perla, Mary Lynch, Eleanor Newhard; Patricia Warner; Kathy Porter; Joey and Renee Spinelli and the gang at Spinelli Graphics; Alison Martin for indexing and research; and finally, Craig Bonner for his off the wall illustrations.

DISCLAIMER

It is not the intent of the author to offer legal advice. For any questions concerning the legality of a situation, occurrence, event or action, you should seek legal counsel from an attorney.

SECRETS OF AN ESTATE-SALE AGENT

FOREWORD

When I was a child, and during the infrequent times my mother left me "home alone" while she ran errands, I delighted in rummaging through her bureau drawers, poking around and trying on jewelry (Where DID that string of jet beads go?) and just plain snooping. It wasn't until several years later when reminiscing with a friend about our childhoods, I discovered she had had no such inclination to snoop when left alone. I began asking other friends and found out only a few of them had this urge to pry like I did. So, with this inherent trait emerging, I didn't become a private eye - I became an estate-sale agent.

If you, too, find this work to your liking, but experience guilt while reading another person's personal papers and need moral justification for snooping, consider the service you are performing. In many cases, you are creating order out of chaos. You can think of it as a giant treasure hunt or, as a fellow "junker" told me, "You are the ultimate recycler".

This is intended to be a "How to...." book, whether for one sale or for many. But after reading it, you may instead want to contact my publisher, screaming, "Get me the author!"

If you still want to learn by doing, proceed carefully. The terrain is full of land mines as well as gold mines.

Chapter 1

WHAT IS AN ESTATE SALE?

1. It is the appraising, pricing, marketing and selling of a person's entire household effects; furniture, appliances, tools, bric-a-brac, sporting goods, antiques, clothing, jewelry and junk. It begins with Autos and continues through Zebra collections.

2. It is not a garage sale, although it probably will include the garage and all it's contents after you've trashed half of it. In a garage sale, you're selling selected items. In an estate sale, you're generally emptying a property.

3. It is advertised in the estate-sale section of the local newspaper where a Wednesday-through-Saturday ad can cost one hundred and fifty to two hundred dollars or more.

4. It generally will be held on Friday (dealers are out buying) and Saturday (half-price day), not Saturday and Sunday as are most garage sales.

5. It can be in a home or apartment (anywhere accessible to the public) or by appointment in a restricted sale area.

Chapter 2

WHY HAVE AN ESTATE SALE

It seems most people assume an estate-sale agent holds sales only for people who have died. Not so. Probably half my sales are for people who have moved out of the area, the state, or into a retirement community. In many cases, they may be very much alive, but you'll never meet them. The son, daughter, or other heir is your contact. In many ways, this is best. It often is an emotional scene to watch as an elderly client comes back for that last look at the former home.

If anyone should ever ask me (nobody has, yet) about the advisability of relocating an aged parent, I'd say sometimes I feel that **if** Dad or Mom can manage alone, it may be best not to uproot them. I've had several ninety-year-olds who lived only a few months after being moved to a new environment. One sweet ninety-two-year-old gentleman kept referring to his wife as we went from one lovely room to another.

"Did she pass away recently?" I asked.

"Oh, no. It's been five years now." He answered, seemingly embarrassed. He appeared quite sound of body, and I think the lingering aura of his departed mate in his familiar surroundings was the stimulus that kept him active and alert. I read his obituary in my weekly community paper exactly two months later.

On the other hand, some elderly people look at relocation as an adventure; they even instigate it. These oldsters, mainly women, are a joy to work with. I especially remember one cute, tiny, Jewish lady who planned everything herself; organized the move, employed me, and sat through all the disorganization and disruption at her home and the frenzy of the two sale days. She seemed to be enjoying it as a new experience. She was moving from California to Florida, along with her fifty-five-year-old daughter.

"Why do you want to move, Regina? You have such a lovely home."

"I want my daughter to find a husband for herself," she answered.

Over lunch (the only client who has ever fed me), she confided that she could die happy when her daughter, who had been divorced twenty years, was remarried. When I pointed out the likelihood that her daughter might be enjoying her single state and her very good job in Los Angeles, and that she, at eighty-three with her great personality, might be the one to find romance in Florida, she giggled, and assured me that after burying two husbands, she was VERY happy living without a man.

"Who loved who the most in that family?" I wondered.

Chapter 3

THE INTERVIEW

You come home from shopping one morning and your answering machine light is flashing. You replay the messages and the last one is: "My name is Viola Green. Please call me at 555-5934. I want to find out about having a sale." Oftentimes callers want to sell just one or two items, but THIS call was an example of why you have an answering machine.

I have learned when people are shopping for someone to hold their sale, they go down a list of available estate agents, and whomever they reach first has the best chance of getting the job. I run an on-going ad for my services in a weekly newspaper. I hold sales in my own city as well as several adjacent towns. I've even spent the weekend out of town in order to put on a <u>good</u> sale.

Viola Green's call came from within the retirement community where I live. Getting a call close to home is an advantage as I can be at the sale home in five minutes or less.

I called Mrs. Green back to get some details. I usually ask clients where they got my name. Oftentimes, if it isn't from my regular ad, it's a referral from another client or from a real estate agent. Referrals are the easiest interviews. Mrs. Green already knew that I did a good job for her friend, otherwise I probably wouldn't have heard from her.

When I get to her home and go in, I find it filled with some very nice antique furniture and collectibles. My pulse rate increases. I'm excited. I tell myself to relax. I haven't gotten the sale yet, and if I do, I don't know what will be left for me to sell. I introduce myself, give her my card, sit down, and we visit a little. Then I explain how I work, and what dates I have open.

We walk through each room, and I write down what is to be sold and what she's taking to her new home. My conversation goes something like this:

"Here's how I work, Mrs. Green. I will come in, set up the sale, appraise, price and sell your things. I'll dispose of the leftovers to whomever you choose, and I'll empty your house.

I don't clean. You'll receive a list of everything I sold and how much it sold for. I charge thirty percent or three hundred dollars minimum, whichever is more (commission and minimum may vary according to the area, or how busy I am). I'd be glad to give you references."

As you are going from room to room, you ask if you may look inside the cupboards.

Now, here's a SECRET. (Remember the title of this book.) If you've spotted a collectible item on your interview visit by unobtrusive peeping (remember my mother's bureau drawers) don't - I repeat - DON'T do this:

1. pull the "gem" out of it's hiding place;

2. drool on it!

If you do any of the above, nine times out of ten it won't be there when you come back to appraise and price. If the "soon-to-be" client pulls it out and wants your opinion, of course you give it.

"I think it will bring forty-five dollars, but it depends on the market" may be all I need to say. I like to quote prices conservatively, and when the clients see the price you received, they'll be much happier, of course, if it's higher than what you estimated.

One client deliberately tested my knowledge about a Spaghettiware bowl from Italy.

"What do you think this bowl is worth?" he asked. He apparently liked my reply as I got his sale, and made him a lot of money.

Don't go out of your way to give random appraisals. You may not sell it at the price you quote, and you'll end up with "egg on your face".

Sometimes you get the job right then and there. Both of you sign the sales agreement (see end of chapter) and at the bottom under "Other Agreements", you list the items the client is taking - the antique mahogany china closet, the oak roll-top desk, the doll collection and the like. At this point, I say something like this:

"This looks like a very nice sale, Mrs. Green, but when you give me the key next week, I'd like to see it again. If you decide to keep more furnishings for your new home between now and then, I may have to reconsider whether it's worth my time and yours to hold

6

the sale. You know, I need a sale of one thousand dollars to make it worthwhile for each of us."

At this point, Mrs. Green may say, "I'll check with my daughter as to when she can move me, and what she wants for herself."

Offer her some moral support (moving can be traumatic) and ask her to call you by a certain date (be specific) as you'll keep a date open until then. You've already given her your little talk about your minimum charge. Say goodbye.

It's now in the laps of the Gods. Never, never call a prospective client back. It puts you in a lesser position, and in this job, you need to be in control from beginning to end. If you're wishy-washy, you'll get thrown out with the leftovers.

You must be a take-charge person to be able to work with the client, the client's relatives, the customers, clean-up organizations, neighbors, and officials in a retirement community. BE BUSINESSLIKE!

You meet Mrs. Green a week later. The relatives have taken only the items listed and you accept the key. But if a lot of your most saleable pieces are gone, ones you were told were to be sold, you still have the option to turn down the sale at this time.

A case in point. I wasn't wishy-washy here, but one must also be PATIENT AND FLEXIBLE. I hadn't heard from one gentleman after an interview until a Saturday afternoon three weeks later when his daughter-in-law called. Fortunately for him, I was home.

"Hi! This is Julia Jones, Mr. Springs' daughter-in-law. We're moving Dad to Oregon tomorrow and he wants you to do his sale right away. Your agreement is here and signed."

In this case, I was still available. My ego was slightly bent, though. (Why had they taken my services for granted? Who would they have gotten to do the job if I hadn't been home?) I went over, picked up the agreement and key, met the relatives and said goodbye. It turned out to be one of my most successful sales.

This experience helped to remind me that in many cases, I am dealing with very elderly people (Mr. Springs was ninety-two) who are sometimes slow to make decisions. They may be in an emotional state from moving, from the loss of a loved one or from ill health, and are often trying to please a son or daughter. BE PATIENT AND FLEXIBLE!

If you don't sign a client on the first interview, it may be because they want to do one of these things:

1.   call and interview other sale agents;
2.   seek advice from a relative;
3.   do it themselves;
4.   think about it.

1.   **Call other sale agents.** Other agents may charge less than your commission. If your clients are shopping to save five percent, let them. Know your value and don't take less than you're worth.

One gentleman I interviewed was plainly shopping for the best deal and asked to pay less. I said that I would like to have his sale, but that I would not cut my commission. I didn't get the sale. A competitor did, and probably for less. The funny part is that the other agent was unable to hold the sale because the client didn't meet the criteria for a sale in our retirement community. He was going to remodel and wanted all new furnishings. He could
only hold a sale if he were to move out of the community, or died!

2. **Seek advice from a relative.** I encourage a prospective client to check with a family member before

committing to a sale. In many instances, they'll be at the home when you arrive or will be the one you'll work with in the case of a death, or a move to a convalescent hospital.

3. **Do it themselves.** I've given people tips on how to do their own sale if I'm unavailable or if they don't have enough for a sale. Small sales (one thousand dollars) could be held by one person, and it's safe to do this in a gated community.

4. **Think about it.** This is where you remind the client that your calendar is filling up or that you have vacation plans. (Yes, you do have a life!) Be specific about your available dates. Bring your calendar to the interview and ask that they call you by a certain date to let you know one way or the other. They may or may not do this, as in Mr. Springs' case.

On the other hand, there may be several reason why **YOU** may not want a sale. It may be that:

1. there's not enough to sell, or it's mostly junk;
2. you don't have a rapport with the client;
3. it's in a bad neighborhood;
4. it's too dirty. If you still want it, charge more;
5. it's too dangerous. (I turned down a sale because of a spider-infested garage. If I'm not up to it, can I ask my helpers to risk it?)

Remember, the interview is very important in establishing a good working relationship with your client. Other than talking to them by phone, it may be the only time you see them in person. Make it a POSITIVE experience.

Here is a sample of an agreement to use when signing a client:

AUTHORIZATION TO HOLD SALE OF PROPERTY

Date (date agreement is signed)

1. (name of agent/yours) is hereby authorized to hold a sale of the following property:
(furniture and household effects)

2. Located at: (address of property)

3. On the following date(s) (sale dates)

4. A full accounting will be delivered to (name of client) within (hours needed) after completion of the sale.

5. (name of agent/yours) will retain XX % of the GROSS receipts from the sale.

6. (client's name) agrees to provide access to the property address for the purpose of appraising, pricing and marketing of the merchandise for sale on the following date: (date client will give key).

7. The estate sale agent named above (your name) agrees to appraise, price and staff the sale.

8. Advertising costs in the form of (name of newspapers) will be paid by (client's name).

9. (client's name) hereby attests that he/she is the legal owner/trustee, etc. of the herein described property, and has the legal right to authorize its sale.

10. Other agreements: (anything held back from sale, or minimum amount required on certain items, etc.)

(client's information)   (agent's information)

_____   _____
signature   signature

_____   _____
(address)   (address)

_____   _____
(city, state, zip)   (city, state, zip)

_____   _____
(area code and phone)   (area code and phone)

Other information: (client's work phone, if applicable)

_____

_____

_____

_____

Chapter 4

LET'S TALK ABOUT RELATIVES

It's very seldom that there are no surviving relatives. They may seem to come out of the woodwork. Never around while the person was alive, they are "all over the place" once their "loved ones" are dead. It seems the further removed the relatives, the more avaricious.

For example, I signed an agreement for a sale that seemed at first to be very straightforward - two brothers sharing all the possessions equally. The house was to go to a close friend and was crammed with collectibles. When I asked if the brothers had removed what they wanted, they said "Yes."

A few days later, I learned the children of one brother wanted a "few mementos." The night I was to go by to pick up the key, I found a pickup truck parked in front and a son and daughter of the client, plus the husband and wife of each, busily pawing through the

12

household effects.

Somewhat taken aback (remember, no one wanted anything else), I left and said I'd return later that evening when they were finished. I wanted to be sure everything was locked up. I'd had company that Saturday night and it was almost ten o'clock when I stopped by to make sure the house was secured. I saw not only the pickup truck still in front, but a rental truck and most of the furniture sitting on the lawn ready to be loaded. I walked in and declared bitingly, "Well, there's not going to be a hundred dollars worth of stuff left to sell." One of the daughters glanced up from her rummaging and replied, "I hope not." I got the picture, and returned my contract and the key to my ex-client, telling him, "I see that you don't need my services." Meekly, he took back his key.

The moral of this tale is that you're not sure what you have to sell until you see the overloaded car pull out of the driveway. Reserve the right to turn down a gutted sale.

The irony of this story is that two days later, I drove by and found a big pile of unwanted items thrown on the lawn for the trash collectors.

I looked through the "debris" and retrieved an oriental vase. I had a copy from the client of the probate appraisal. Matching up the vase with its description, I saw it was valued at seventy-five dollars. I considered it my "consultation fee."

Here's another example of what can happen:

I had taken a sale based primarily on a very fine mahogany Queen Anne dining set and six matching chairs. Almost all the value of the sale was in these items. When I went in to begin pricing, and after about six hours of work, I returned the next day to find a note on the table stating, "Don't sell this." On calling the client and reminding her that she had said this was to be sold, she said, "But Mother wants her grandson to have this. What can I do?" They've stonewalled you.

What do you do? Ethically, they should pay the commission you have lost. Only a very few clients will do this, but I have had some great ones who left notes and money for even the smallest items they removed after I began my job. Unless you've been quite firm in the beginning, you may be faced with a gutted sale, one step removed from a garage sale. You've already invested your time and cleared your calendar. You may decide to "bite the bullet" and go ahead and hold this pared down sale, but be more careful next time.

"What difference (other than money) does it make?" you may ask. You've got a sale.

This is the difference: while you're doing this sale, you may have turned away a better one. There are only so many weekends you can work, and believe me, two sales a month are a lot. I did one a week for six weeks in a row and almost collapsed. I have a friend who can work this often and thrives on it. I can't.

Remember, this is supposed to be fun. Learn to be selective. It hurts when you are booked and have to refer someone to a competitor, but it works both ways. My friend who works every week, has sent people to me, and I've sent clients to others.

You must remember also that prospective clients don't always think about the necessity of a sale until escrow is about to close, and you're booked.

This is how I found myself working six weeks in a row. Learn to say no.

Unless you have a lot of help and are Charles Atlas, you'll kill yourself. This is very hard physical work.

A good example of my own overkill occurred in my first probate sale. After walking through the apartment with the trust management executor and pulling items she thought the out-of-state heirs would want from their aunt's home (I was to sell everything else), she asked if I could photograph them. The deceased ninety-four-year old aunt had had a treasure trove of old Hummel figurines, Haviland, handpainted china from the 1900's and exquisite cut glass.

I agreed to do it and, although I'd never photographed for a sale, I saw it as a challenge. I had a good time setting up displays on velvet and doing lighting. I was so inspired, I not only photographed the items selected by the executor, but included other things as well, including twenty-six different cups and saucers including several Shelleys, saleable to any dealer at fifty dollars each. Talk about dumb! I did such a great job of photography and display that the heirs, two elderly nephews, wanted it all including the teacups. The only teacups I had left for the sale were four that had been out of camera range.

Monetarily, I did well. I was paid not only my sales commission, but for my photography and all the packing of items shipped to heirs.

But did I really need to include unasked for items? The answer was a resounding "NO."

I had gutted my own sale.

At another time, I held a sale that included a closet of fine men's clothes. The heirs, a son and daughter, told me they were leaving it all for me to sell. I gasped when the son pulled a valuable, designer suit from the closet. Needless to say, that particular piece of finery was not there when I began marking, even though it wasn't the son's size.

Only a row of sad-looking shoes remained - Bally's, Clarks and other imported Italian footwear. They were an odd size and didn't fit any customers. After the sale, I polished these well-worn loafers with care and gave them to a friend to take to homeless men.

Chapter 5

PRICING

Probably one of the questions I'm asked most frequently is "How do you know what amount to price an item?" Experience, experience and more experience is the answer.

I got mine from working alongside another agent. The pragmatic way. I learned (and am learning) by doing. I don't know if this is the best way for everyone. It is for me.

Some of us are born with the ability to know the value of things. Some have to learn it. I think I have a combination of both. I've often felt I was a reincarnated bazaar hawker from Marrakech.

This is a business which requires constant

learning and updating as you go along. Prices and values, of course, are not static or constant. Depression glass may be hot one year and cold the next.

I generally price an everyday item at about a fourth to a third of its retail price. If a new refrigerator of the same general make and model costs six hundred dollars new, then one hundred and fifty to two hundred dollars is a good price for a used one.

Remember to build in some dickering room at this point. If, in your mind, you want around one hundred and eighty dollars for the fridge, mark it at two hundred and twenty-five dollars. This will give everyone enough bargaining space to get you to your goal. I build in a fairly standard twenty percent on big items, especially if they're things people always need. The condition of the item you're selling and the neighborhood where the sale is being held have a great deal to do with whether you get your price. Sometimes you can't sell an item at any price even on half-price day, but sell it you must. Remember you're emptying the house.

One thing you absolutely must remember during the two sale days is: DO NOT GET DISCOURAGED. It's easy to become crestfallen when you're looking at eight pieces of large furniture at noon of the second day. Stay in the present. Pay no attention to the "doom and gloom" people wandering in and out. (This is one reason you want the clients elsewhere on sale days.) If you keep a positive and optimistic attitude, then, nine times out of ten, someone will come in and buy. You may not sell some of the furniture for much, but you'll get it out of the house. A little creative bookkeeping will cover the fact that the almost new four hundred dollar lounge chair priced at one hundred dollars sold for only forty dollars. (See chapter on Sale Days.)

PRICING SOURCES

1. Newspapers - The Sunday papers, in particular the ads for stereo, TVs, appliances, and furniture.
2. Current department store catalogs - Sears, Best, etc.
3. Other agents in the business.
4. Antique malls.
5. Furniture stores.
6. Telephone - A call to a furniture store salesman about. a maker or line of merchandise may get you the information you need without a trip.
7. Books - The yearly <u>SCHROEDER'S ANTIQUES PRICE GUIDE COLLECTOR BOOKS</u> Order from: P.O. Box 3009, Paducah, Kentucky 42002-3009, or call to order toll free at 1-800-626-5420. Cost is $14.95 plus $2 shipping. With a resale number and a six book order, you get a discount. Every year the guide is updated. You might keep the last three and sell older ones. This is the guide I use most.

I also have <u>KOVELS ANTIQUES AND COLLECTIBLES PRICE LIST</u> ($14.95). This is published by Crown and sells in bookstores, as well as through Collector Books. It's a smaller guide, but I find the print a little too small to read easily.

I have about thirty books. You'll acquire books as the need arises. I have quite a few jewelry guides, as this is an area of much interest to me. (See chapter on Jewelry)

8. Shopping other estate sales.
9. Libraries - You don't always have to buy the book.
10. Classes - University or private, especially for gemology courses.
11. Discount stores - Target, WalMart, K Mart. I particularly check their kitchenware and linens. I'm

appalled at the prices. I mark one-fourth of the store prices; however, customers balk at anything over fifty cents. If I've marked a Pyrex measuring cup at one dollar and it costs four dollars at a discount store, I may have to wait to sell it for half price on the second day. If they complain, and they do, my reply may be, "Have you checked the price at the store lately?" Yes, they have and that's why they're shopping your sales.

Chapter 6

SETTING UP THE SALE

To set up a sale, you are going to create chaos out of order. Let me explain. You will, in an ideal situation, enter a house in which the heirs have already taken the family mementos and certain antiques, and have declared, "We're through! Here's the key."

You must then create space by moving the remaining furniture to make room for your card tables, which are a part of your tools of the trade. (See chapter on Tools of the Trade.) You should close off a room if you can, making it easier to monitor your merchandise.

I always post a "KEEP OUT" sign on the bathroom door. This is where you will keep your supplies and personal belongings. (Purses, however, go under your sales table.) Now the fun begins.

You and any helpers you have coerced by bribery, lunch, on-the-job training or (if all else fails) money, pull everything from cupboards, dresser drawers and closets and organize it. All the pretty things (china, crystal, teacups, figurines) may go on two, three or more card tables covered with your lace table cloth. Kitchenware will go on the kitchen counters, and as many pots and pans as possible will be piled up on the stove.

I recall one of my earliest sales. I had been interviewed by the lady and her sister the week before, gotten the job, and returned for the key to find that they had packed ALL the sale items into large boxes and put them on the floor. They had doubled my work! Now instead of standing and pulling down shelf items to the counter, I had to lift boxes from the floor or, equally as bad, to work on the floor.

ALWAYS tell your clients to leave everything as it is, and you'll be more than glad to do the throwing away. This also includes food. For example, almost all partially used spices can be sold, if people are not too finicky. Fifty cents for a jar three-fourths full of marjoram is a bargain compared to two dollars and a half at the market. Don't, however, sell paprika. It gets buggy.

You doing the trashing is important for another reason. Most people don't know what is saleable; and, if not cautioned, will throw away hundreds of dollars of good stuff - - -   pocket knives along with pill bottles, old perfume vials along with used makeup, even good jewelry along with old, rotting thread.

As you go from room to room with a large trash bag, you separate trash from treasures. For instance, your clients are the heirs of a deceased ninety-three-year-old woman. In many cases, the older the deceased, the more likely that the collectibles (and these are your priority items) have been moved up, up and finally out of the house. This woman may have owned and used Bauer, Catalina, or Metlox pottery as her everyday dishes fifty years ago. More often, it's been "upgraded" to Noritake, stoneware or plastic. If the heirs haven't had an eye on the old pottery, it's been packed away.

One lady split a beautiful and valuable set of Winchester pattern Johnson Bros. china to give to a friend, keeping a few odd pieces for herself. I've found an entire set of Franciscan pottery relegated to an outdoor closet on a patio.

If the choicest pieces haven't been on display, then the highest, most inaccessible shelf in the kitchen or the very farthest reaches of the pots and pans cupboard is where you'll find granny's oversized, perfect, cut glass pitcher, her rarely used Bavarian china soup tureen, or a twenty-two inch Limoges platter.

I have a dear friend who works with me on occasion. She loves to decorate and to do store display, and she's very good at it. In order not to hurt her feelings, I let her "do her thing", setting up attractive furniture arrangements and table displays.

My customers don't need or want a beautiful setting. They like a jumble of goods they can root through, the messier the better for most people. The exception, I've found, is crystal and bric-a-brac. You can often get a better price after you've washed those fifty-year-old goblets that have been on that top shelf for twenty years.

Be sure Cable TV boxes, or any borrowed or rented equipment such as wheelchairs or walkers, are returned to the proper party. This is the client's responsibility, but they may enlist your help.

In some situations, the heirs are unable to remove the furniture they're keeping until after the sale. If this is the case, simply cover the item with a sheet and mark it "Not For Sale". Be sure it's a fairly large sign, otherwise the customer will be peeking under the sheet. If you have an empty room other than the bathroom where you can store it, so much the better.

The towels and sheets and fine linens should be folded onto the beds or card tables. Strip the beds in order to show the mattresses. Beds aren't the easiest things to sell. In one instance, though, I got lucky and sold four twin beds to two young men who were furnishing a half-way house for recovering alcoholics.

Oftentimes, a household will include many of the cleaning items and supplies you'll need to set up a sale. I tell my client, "I don't clean a house. I empty it." In some situations, however, you must clean at least part of it in order to set it up. This is especially true in the kitchen and bathroom. You will be using the bathroom, and you may want a cup of coffee from the kitchen while you're working. Some agents charge a higher commission for a dirty house, and some don't take the sale. I've done neither. Perhaps I've been lucky in not getting a really dirty one. Spiders I may refuse, but so far I've braved dirt.

Wear an apron and old clothes, a cap or scarf, and surgical gloves (for bathrooms, kitchens and tool sheds). The gloves are well worth the effort it takes to get used to them. I had to give up wearing contact lenses because of the dirt and dust. Remember, you may be disturbing twenty or more years of dirt. If you're into having nice finger-nails, this isn't the business for you.

I prefer going through the half-used makeup in bathroom drawers in the hopes of finding a treasure rather than asking the relatives of the deceased to empty them. Some relatives have done it before they called you. Others are not about to. In a typical sale, I'll probably trash hundreds of dollars worth of makeup and drugs (down the toilet), none of which I resell. Unopened, non-prescription drugs and make-up are OK to sell. Check expiration dates.

I stopped putting stickers on kitchen utensils because they come off too easily. If I could staple into plastic, I would. Instead, I now use a grease pencil or black marker as often as I can. Very small items such as corn holders or nutcrackers and small office supplies I will bundle together into a baggie and will staple it closed, pricing the bag. It's sold all or nothing.

You'll need lots of plastic grocery bags and newspapers to wrap small things. I get my bags from the recycle containers in front of markets. If you can't find the container and have to ask, go somewhere else. They probably don't want you to take them.

The time you spend pricing and setting up may take anywhere from four to one hundred or more hours. Keep your pricing guides at hand, and do the difficult pricing like collectibles when you're the freshest and sharpest.

I use the reward system by interspersing work I like with yucky tasks. If I've had to trash a very dirty bathroom, I'll treat myself to pricing a pile of beautiful old lace.

You'll need to carefully sort through papers if the heirs haven't already done so. Anything you think is important or valuable, put in a box and leave in the bathroom for your client. Old photographs, color slides, documents and albums belong in this category. I'm constantly amazed at how much memorabilia relatives DON'T want. I guess they couldn't trash it and want a stranger to do it. Oftentimes, I've left a box full of personal items with a note, only to find the box still there after the sale. In one instance where I'd done a total of three sales for the same woman, I discovered the same box of her father's World War II documents, discharge papers, and medical history in a closet when I completed her sale. At that point, I felt so attached to the family, it was even hard for me to consign a lifetime to the trash heap.

A word to the wise. When you've accepted a job and begin setting up, you may look at the task before you and wonder how you will ever plow through the mountain of possessions facing you. DON'T THINK. JUST BEGIN.

I had a wonderful sale in a tiny, one bedroom, detached cottage in a poor neighborhood. The man had numerous hobbies. Every nook and cranny was crammed with goodies. He made candy and confections and canned. He had the biggest assortment of Christmas decorations I'd ever seen; plate collections, woodworking tools, and on and on. Why did I take it? It was also crammed with collectibles and extremely clean, although you simply couldn't move. I turned off my brain and sat down in the furthest corner of the teensy-weensy kitchen and began pulling cans from cupboards. He had enough food for two years. I just worked my way out of the house. On sale day, we could only let 10 people in at a time. I set up sawhorses and planks in the yard for the hundreds of Christmas decorations. It was a huge success.

Specialized Marking Techniques
To set up sets of dishes, you must examine each and every piece by sight and feel. What defects you can't see, you may feel as you run your fingers around the edges. Hold them to the light and look for cracks and crazing (minute cracks in the glaze). If a piece is cracked, it will sound dead. Stack the china and price it as a set. Always try to sell your sets as sets. Customers, especially dealers, may want to buy specific pieces such as any or all of the serving pieces. These items

command the highest prices and are easily sold. Near the end of the sale, you may have to break up the set in order to sell it. Sometimes the price you get for the serving pieces alone amounts to the price of an entire set. I've acquired a few partial sets of beautiful china in this way. Tally the set on a separate sheet of paper, and put it with the dishes. For example, "dinner plates; good - 8, as-is - 2". Add up all the perfect pieces in one column and the as-is in another column, and put the price for the set at the top.

When examining crystal stemware, run your fingers around the edge, look, and also ring it. If it's not damaged, it will have a bell-like tone. Price crystal as sets also. Your price will vary according to the quality of the crystal. For example, Waterford brings the highest price.

Problems During Setup and Sale Days
During the setting up of a few of my sales, I've had to work around people who were still living in the house. In my very first sale, the couple (the wife had some obscure illness) assured me they would stay out of the way in their upstairs bedrooms. As most of the furnishings upstairs were spoken for, I didn't see this as a   problem. They promised me they'd be gone the days of the sale when, as I told them, "controlled mayhem would occur." Not only did this couple never leave the house during the setup, but they were very much in evidence on both sale days, drinking cup after cup of coffee and both smoking like steam engines. This certainly didn't help.

Why do you want clients "away" on sale days? In most cases, they are the "kiss of death". At the least, they send tense vibes that any would-be buyer can pick up. They hover. I tell them, "It's your sale, and you have the right to be here, but I can sell a whole lot better alone."

The second worst situation to having your clients, who are obviously the owners, standing around, is to have a next-door neighbor popping in at frequent intervals moaning, "Oh, the cherry dining set is still here. Do you think you can sell it?" It's only two hours into the first day, and she's determined to scotch your sale. She probably wants it herself for half price or, even more likely, as a gift. My answer, through a fixed smile, is a firm, "I intend to." as I head her toward the nearest exit.

Chapter 7

SALE DAYS

Day One

The morning of the sale you'll probably be up by five-thirty. If you haven't made your sandwiches the night before, the wise thing to do, then you have a lunch to make for yourself and whoever is helping you. Your help can vary from you alone to seven or more people. I provide at least a sandwich apiece, plus a few more. Add soft drinks and some cookies for snacks and you're ready. On very large sales, I've used a nearby restaurant to cater lunch.

You will have signs to put up (see chapter on Advertising) so you should be out of the house before 7 A.M. If you can arrange to have one of your salespeople ride with you, this will speed up this process. It takes about twenty minutes to post signs. On your way to work each day, you will have scouted the neighborhood and know which are the best and busiest corners on which to place them.

If your sale starts at 8 A.M., you should arrive a half hour early. This gives you ample time to set the stage - open drapes, light rooms, locate your favorite radio music station on your own portable radio, and let your helpers shop. This may be the first time some of them have had the opportunity to buy. Be sure you tell them to come early.

When you drive up, you should see a nice long line in front of the door, plus cars cruising by. Put your car in the driveway when there is one. Make note of street sweeping days, and place a sign on the door if possible. After a few sales in your city, you'll see many familiar faces. The regulars include dealers, collectors and shop owners.

Greet them and tell them you'll open just as soon as you can get ready. They love it if you open five or ten minutes ahead of time. This enables them to get a jump on the next sale on their list.

Your designated entrance will vary. It's usually through the front door, but in several instances, I've routed customers through the garage first if it's attached. Keep in mind that, if it is possible to arrange, you want only **ONE** entrance and exit. Your cashiers will be there. If there's a detached garage, close the gate across the driveway, if there is one, and route "shoppers" through the front door.

You've now set the stage and it's time to open the curtain. The crowd is eager and ready to shop. Occasionally, you'll find someone trying to sneak in through a side gate. Shoo them firmly back into line. It's a jungle out there, but hopefully there's some sort of pecking order, and you're safely behind doors for the moment. Some sales agents give out numbers to organize their crowds. I have never felt it necessary to do this, and my customers tell me they don't like being numbered.

When I open the door, I always stand at the entrance dispensing cheery "good mornings", and admonish all to be polite and to have fun; a leftover from my school marm years. Even adults need to be reminded that courtesy is best - most especially collectors. The last thing you want is a riot on your hands. This is the reason that when you think enough customers are in the house, have someone at the door to hold back the crowd, or say "You'll have to wait a few minutes", and shut the door; making sure it's locked. As most thefts occur in this first rush of business, you must be extremely alert. You may need to hire a security guard if you are selling a large amount of valuable items.

A word here about YOUR special duties.

You, as the person in charge, will be all over the place (I only cashier on small sales). You will be negotiating prices, watching the crowd and merchandise and answering LOTS of questions.

You will have assembled your help before you open the front door and given them a little pep talk. Remind them you've priced in a twenty percent bargaining amount on the large items (see chapter on Pricing) and encourage them to SELL.

Tell your salespeople there is no bargaining on low priced items. Tell your cashiers that their job is to take money and keep records, and not to allow customers to attempt to bargain with them. If you're working alone, then, of course, you have to do it all.

In special cases, for instance, where you have lots of garage and garden items and don't want them hauled in the house, you have several options.

Let your garage salesperson take the money to a cashier and return with the customer's change. (He can step ahead of the line, if necessary.) Be sure your salesperson makes note of the item and the amount on a slip of paper and gives it to the cashier, who can enter the transaction later on the sales sheet.

Or, the garage salesperson can write the item up and send the customer inside to pay. The cashier takes the money, marks the slip "Paid", and the customer returns to drag off the chaise lounge or dirty tool bench.

Lastly, the garage salesperson can make change from his apron pocket (all helpers wear work aprons), and you can pick up the money and lists at frequent intervals.

If the checkout line is very long, and hopefully it will be, go up and down and let the customers pay you for one or two small items. Most customers don't like to wait very long. They probably have more sales to shop. You're the ringmaster, and instead of a whip, you can keep them all happy with a little humor and cheerfulness.

Be sure your sales people have plenty of price stickers, as well as pens and paper, in their sales aprons. I use the brightest colored stickers I can find; orange and yellow are the most noticeable. You may need to restaple a price sticker to the sleeve of some of the clothing or the linens. I thought I was discouraging customers from removing price stickers from these items when I began stapling them on. Some clothes or linens still arrive at the checkout table with only the staple remaining. I guess the would-be bargain hunters didn't want to ruin their fingernails.

Loudly, I may say something like: "Oh, the sticker is gone! If I have to reprice it, I usually mark it higher as I'm not in my Alpha state. (Your customers expect you to be a little weird. It comes with the job.) Or, I'll put the item behind the checkout table and announce, "It will have to wait until I'm not so busy." Such a harsh reaction slows down the annoying ploy of price-sticker removal.

I'd like to mention here the use of several colors of stickers. In some sales, other family members have brought in things to be sold. This can add to your sale and your commission. Be sure not to accept junk. Many of these people will just put it all in Grandma's pot, as they may be dividing an inheritance equally. Some clients want the goods separated. A different color sticker achieves this result. On the sales sheet at the table, the cashier can write the color to one side. This is extra work for you so be sure you explain it to your client and do it only if it's profitable and if you're able to handle the resulting extra work.

In setting up a sale, I try to use as few card tables as I can get by with. When the goods on them become sparse, I consolidate. Fold up your tables as they are emptied, and put them in the "KEEP OUT" bathroom. You want your sale to appear as full as possible. As you sell the furniture in a room, move the smaller pieces out into another room and close off the empty one.

You'll start each day of your sale with one hundred and seventeen dollars in your till. If you have more than one cashier, they will each have this amount in their own till. When you have a big sale with a jewelry table, you'll have another till. A collection of jewelry for sale creates a high intensity area and breeds the greatest chance for theft. Put your most alert, sharp and trustworthy sales people at the jewelry table. Don't have your customers floating around with handfuls of jewelry they intend to buy. Either keep it for them at the checkout table where the jewelry may be or have them, in a big sale, pay at the jewelry table and then continue shopping. Bag it for them and mark "Paid" on the bag. A courteous, "I'll hold the ring for you while you shop, " is often all you need to say. I've only had one or two customers take this as a personal affront on their integrity. Compared to the many who have walked out with these small things without paying, this is a plus.

I prefer this assortment of bills and coins for my sales.

25 dollar bills	=	$25.00
11 five dollar bills	=	$55.00
2 ten dollar bills	=	$20.00
1 roll quarters	=	$10.00
1 roll of dimes	=	$5.00
1 roll nickels	=	$2.00
		$117.00

You, or your cashier, should write down the amount an item brought on lined scratch pads. You only give a receipt on a deposit item. I'll discuss this in detail further on. In some cases, you should be aware of a minimum amount a client expects to get for an item. When this occurs, you have two options. You may call them at the end of the first day and tell them what is left, and remind them that tomorrow is half price day. They'll tell you to either sell it or save it for them. They may have use for it themselves.

Your second option, if they say "Sell" and you still can't get half price, is to use your miscellaneous entries. You will have, over the course of two days, listed some items as miscellaneous. These are usually odds and ends of kitchenware or linens, or all that loose change you've accumulated for small, low price items. The majority of things sold will be listed descriptively on your sales sheets; for example "sofa - $50", or "china closet - $200".

Now, total up all the miscellaneous at the end of each day (it adds up) and see how much money you have to "spend". This is where a little creative bookkeeping comes in. (Remember the book title.)

If, by every sales trick in your book, you just managed to sell that sofa for only twenty dollars (you were lucky to sell it at all), by using the miscellaneous amounts, you can adjust the sale price to forty-five dollars. Do this if you feel the client would be upset by learning the actual amount received.

During your initial interview, you already paved the way to reality when you were straightforward concerning the price a piece of furniture might bring. Twenty-five percent of retail is fair, taking into account age and wear. Antiques present a different story.

Antiques and collectibles will be scarce at most of your sales.

Be reluctant to take deposits on things unless you know the customers, or feel strongly that they will be back within the time you've given them (usually an hour) to pay the balance.

When you've accepted a deposit, you've pulled the merchandise from the sale, and it may have been a most wanted item that is easily sold and well priced. Help the buyers locate the nearest automatic teller machine (ATM), wrap their money in a receipt, and place it in the bottom of the till. For example: "Mrs. Jones paid $20 cash on a $120 dresser". Sign it and date it. Give the customer a copy of the receipt. This way, when they return, you can easily pull out the deposit and slip, and complete the sale. Keeping this separately helps eliminate errors. You are working under a great deal of pressure, and customers may be excited about their purchases. They may even want to exchange an earlier check deposit for cash. Cash is always most desirable.

If a depositor hasn't returned in the time allotted, you'll be within your rights to put the merchandise back up for sale. When a large piece of furniture has been paid for and isn't moved at time of purchase, put a SOLD and PAID sticker on it with the buyer's name and phone number. Don't write SOLD on anything until you have received all the sale price. Caution your sales force about this. When, in the first rush of a sale, a customer says, "I want the chest of drawers", ask the customer to "please pay for it now" then urge them to continue shopping. You may be paid directly. Be careful because often there will be a change of mind. Some dealers, who should know better, change their minds as much as any other customers. The practice removes the item from the market during the peak hours when you should be able to get the best price.

I allow myself forty-eight hours (and I write this into the agreement) to give the client the final sales outcome, although I always call at the end of the first day with an approximate total. The customer doesn't have to know what something sold for. "I got my price, " is a good answer. Even, "I forget" is a nice way of saying, "It's not necessarily your business." The client always needs to know and as quickly as possible. I give myself the forty-eight hours because I do the bookkeeping after selling all day. You may have someone tallying and writing up totals as the sale progresses. This is a good idea if you have the time. Don't get sidetracked from selling to do accounts. First things first - SELL, SELL, SELL.

Your sales sheets belong to only you and your client. For your eyes only is a good credo. On occasion, a customer will try to find out what something was sold for by peeking over the cashier's shoulder. They wanted it at a certain price and want to make sure someone didn't out-bargain them. Don't allow this to happen!

Your final task, at the end of the first day, is to organize the remaining merchandise for the next day, pay your help, and go home, and relax and start writing up your first day's sales.

Day Two

The second day of a sale looks and feels, as it should, totally different from Day One. First, there won't be much of a line at the door, if there is one at all. You won't need to get there in the "wee hours" either. On your way to the job, go by all of the signs you posted if you didn't do it when you left the day before. If some have been removed, and you have extras, replace them.

The early arrivals probably will be customers that saw something they wanted the first day, but waited for the price to be halved. The truly confident shoppers will wait until the final hour of the second day, when the prices are even lower.

You'll work almost as hard on the second day as you did on the first, but will make much less money for it - one fourth to one third of the first day's amount. This allows you to cut down on your second day's hours.

You can definitely cut back on help. One extra helper may be all you need. Keep in mind their pay comes off the top of your commission. You may even be able to close early. If you're down to two boxes of odds and ends, and a tired sofa and old chair, you've done well. Put a sign on the door that says "Sold Out' or leave your phone number on the door and the drapes open. If anyone comes by and is interested, they'll call. Otherwise it is ready for the cleanup organization to pick up.

Dress for comfort on both sale days. Really good athletic shoes are a must, along with your best work apron.

Be "laid back" if you like, but BE IN CHARGE.

The final task after all the rooms are empty and picked up and final trash dumped, is to pick up your signs from the corners.

Congratulations!

You've done it!

Not quite. You still have your records to finish and checks to make out before you can pay yourself.

Chapter 8

LEFTOVERS AND CLEANUP

The most frequently asked question I hear from both clients and customers is, "What do you do with the leftovers after the sale?"

Ideally, there will be none. In an imperfect world, this perfect solution isn't always achieved, but the property must be emptied, one way or another. The leftovers may range from two boxes of assorted kitchenware and linens and no furniture, to enough stuff for a garage sale. You can do one of these things:

Give Away Leftovers or Donate Them

I ask my clients which charitable organization they would like to help out. If they belong to a church, or service group, this may be where they will want leftovers to wind up. In some instances, they may already have made arrangements. If they don't have a preference, or if they live in another state, I will make suggestions. Ask your clients their preferences before you make suggestions. You want to assure them there are no hidden dealings, and that you have no tie-in with any particular group. If clients don't care where their dad's clothes go, I will suggest some options. My favorite disposition is to give clothing to a woman who personally distributes it to either homeless men, battered women's groups, or fire or flood victims. Discuss this with the clients. Some sons and daughters may not like the idea of a homeless man wearing one of dad's suits. Then, other offspring may think this is exactly what dad would have wanted.

The Goodwill, Salvation Army, Purple Heart Veterans and Christian Outreach are a few of the many organizations that will pick up leftovers. They, in turn, sell the goods in their stores or give them away. Be sure to find out if they take "the bitter with the better." I've had mattresses and bulky things left with a note that the organization either doesn't need it, or it's not good enough. If this happens, I stop giving to these groups. There is a lot of money to be made by the groups that collect leftovers. It makes your work harder if you have to arrange for two separate pick-ups.

Most nonprofit groups will give you a receipt to authenticate an income tax deduction. You usually fill in the amount or value of the donated items. The estate-sale agent should take care of this for the client. I tell the client what I estimate the value to be, and let them fill it in. I collect the receipt and mail it to the client.

If a sale is very small, or of little value, it may be to the owners' advantage to donate it and take a tax write-off. This situation may arise when there are lawyers, or probate involved.

Buy It Myself

In many instances, I buy the leftovers for myself or for someone in my family. But just how many lovely sofas can you put into an 800-square-foot apartment?

In one sale, I had an entire set of Heywood-Wakefield furniture - sofa, three chairs, coffee table and bedroom dressers and headboards. All were collectible and in excellent condition. I advertised it for sale with care, called every dealer I could think of who might be interested, but - nothing. It was in the wrong place at the wrong time. At the time of the sale, blonde Heywood-Wakefield was very hot - not so, cherry. I ended up selling all the living room furniture for a song (around three hundred dollars) to a young collector at the "eleventh hour" of the second day. A dealer's trick - see it on Day One, buy it at 3 P.M. on Day Two. My daughter bought the dresser, and it's the best piece of furniture in her home.

Six months later, I called the young dealer (he had become a regular at my sales after this) to see if he'd sell me back the couch. It was a lovely piece and I'd decided to get rid of another sofa to accommodate it, but we never came to an agreement on the price. He was still trying to double his money. He called me some months later to see if I still wanted the sofa as he hadn't been able to sell it. In the meantime, I had purchased an antique Eastlake settee and couldn't use it. Needless to say, my home has an eclectic assortment of furnishings that I've "rescued". Not running a mall space or antique shop, I must constantly take care not to turn my "digs" into a storage locker.

41

Sell It

In the case of a very large sale, this can not only get the property emptied, but can add a few more dollars to the total sale. Some clients feel good about donating, while others feel better about making another dollar or two. Over the years, I've used a young couple not only to help me set up and work the sale, but to handle the leftovers. He, in turn, takes them to his neighborhood and holds his own garage sale. I'm sure this has helped him in a large way to support his big family. This is the hardest, dirtiest, most labor intensive part of this job, so be generous. Sell the cleanup man the leftovers cheap. Fifty to one hundred dollars is tops.

I used Bill in my very first sale to work and clean up. There was a nice clean sofa that I couldn't sell at any price the first or second day. (Sofas are probably the most difficult thing to sell.) After negotiating his clean-up fee for the leftovers, we pulled it outside. As Bill was moving it onto the sidewalk to put onto his truck, a man strolled by.

"How much do you want for that sofa?" he inquired.

"Fifty dollars", Bill answered. The man bought in on the spot. For two days, we hadn't been able to sell it, even when it was reduced to twenty-five dollars on the second day. We laughed and decided we should have pulled ALL the leftovers onto the lawn! The client who had remained through both sale days and heard this story was a little chagrined. This is a good reason why you want your client to see only the empty house and the check. They don't need to see all the "in-between."

For me, a good cleanup man is better than a cleanup organization. A good cleanup man will do a lot of the things you would have to do yourself to get the leftovers ready for the nonprofit organization to pick up.

A good cleanup man will arrive at the time you specify (around two p.m. on the last day) with boxes and a dolly, and will pack up everything you tell him to pack. He'll also go through the house and see that it's empty. You'll need to follow him to see that he doesn't take things you've bought, or your own supplies. He'll haul away industrial products and old boxes of scrap iron and metal - things that a nonprofit group won't take.

A good cleanup man knows his worth and is very independent. If you can find one who is reliable, on time, hard working and fairly honest (only takes what you tell him to), he is worth his weight in gold. That is the main reason you don't charge him a lot for those leftovers. He will, in turn, resell them.

You don't want to ask what they do with what they buy, though. I used a great one for some time until he was put out of business by a neighborhood complaint to the city. It seems he had turned his residential property into a giant junk yard.

Cleanup is a very important part of a sale. It's also one in which many agents fall short. Even though you and your client have been paid, you are not finished until the house and garage are emptied.

Chapter 9

RECORD KEEPING AND THINGS LEGAL

You as an estate sale agent can act as crazy as you like, as long as you can make change quickly and accurately and keep good records. If you can't keep records, hire a trusted cashier. Using your own son, daughter, husband or wife is best. There's a lot of money involved, and you are accountable.

This might be the place to discuss just how binding, on either party, the initial sales agreement may be. I've never had to test this in court. If potential clients change their minds and decide against a sale, I would simply drop it and bid my adieu. I strive to avoid things legal.

I am, however, more concerned whether my client is still carrying homeowners' liability insurance on the property. I'm vastly more worried about being sued by an injured customer than in suing a client who reneges on a sale.

In a retirement community, the odds are that there is still insurance in effect. Where a property has been closed for months, you'll be fortunate to have electricity, let alone liability insurance. Be sure you ask about this during your initial interview. Be very cautious even if there is insurance. There are a lot of hazards lying loose around a sale - knives, sharp objects, etc. because you've pulled everything out of hiding places. I keep pocket knives and scissors at my check-out table for safety (and to prevent theft). The garage is an especially dangerous area. I remember one young mother who turned her two-year old loose in the back yard where numerous attractive hazards were within reach. Finally, she left reluctantly after I asked her several times to watch her child. I guess we were the babysitters for the afternoon. Say something like, "Watch your child", and look like a playground director as you look them in the eye. You also need to pay extra attention to the very old. I have one almost blind lady who comes to my sales. I breathe a sign of relief when I've helped Ruth out the door. I've even taken her home when she seemed to be especially tottery.

When you get home, transfer all figures from your scratch sheets (only you can read them anyway) to eight and a half by eleven, yellow lined paper with an adding machine tape attached to each page. Send all the sheets (there will be a lot) with your cover letter, showing totals less your commission. Show your arithmetic on this paper as it will head off any argument.

Deposit all checks to your own account as they're made out to you. You have written the customer's driver's license number and work phone number on the check so that you can collect from them if the check bounces. Finally, write the client a check on your own account.

My bookkeeping and accounting passed muster on

my second sale. It was for a retired chief executive officer (CEO) in charge of finance for a large West Coast airplane manufacturer. He thanked me and said, "Anytime you need a letter of reference, have your client call me. I'd be glad to give you a good one."

That was compliment enough. He was one of my clients who fulfilled all the duties of a client and added some pleasurable ones. He'd leave me in his lovely home to work alone and to be guarded by his friendly toy poodle, Charlie.

If you're only going to do a sale for yourself, or on an infrequent schedule, you probably can avoid city licenses and permits. Every city will have it's own rules so be sure you find out what they are. Be sure you pay your fair share of any taxes on your profits. This includes federal and state income taxes, as well as sales tax. Check with your local franchise tax board on the method they want you to use for collecting sales tax.

If you grow big, get an accountant.

Chapter 10

ADVERTISING AND MARKETING

Ads

Advertising can be expensive if it is printed in a daily newspaper. When I first began holding sales, I paid a percentage of the ad equal to my sales commission. If I charged twenty-five percent commission on the sale, I paid twenty-five percent of the cost of the ad. You may do this if you feel it's fairer, but I now charge the entire ad fee to the client and I have never had a complaint. In fact, when I paid part of it, the client seemed surprised.

A daily paper will bill me a week or so later for the ad. The least my client has spent advertising in a daily paper for a four day ad running Wednesday through

Saturday is seventy-five dollars, the most was three hundred dollars. A rule of thumb: only mention a particular item if it's priced at fifty dollars or more. If you're selling an auto, piano or organ, it's a good idea to also place a small inexpensive ad in those classified sections of the paper. At the end of the sale, all advertising costs are taken from the amount paid to the client.

I held one very large sale in an area that was on the edge of two cities. I placed ads in six different publications for a total of four hundred and fifty dollars. This was at the suggestion of my client and with his approval. Be sure you have a clear understanding with the client as to what and where you intend to advertise.

In my daily city paper, there will be only about four to six sales listed each week, sometimes only one or two. DON'T let the telephone salesperson coax you into placing a CHEAPER garage-sale ad. Insist on the ESTATE SALE classification, and pay the much higher charge. You'll draw a completely different kind of buyer, one that is prepared to spend more. There will be dozens of ads under the GARAGE-SALE section. Just be sure you are holding an estate sale and not a garage sale (Reread Chapter Two: What is an Estate Sale.)

Here is an ad I placed in a daily newspaper:
(This was a few years ago, and rates may have changed since then. There were only two ads under the Estate-Sale classification. My ad ran four days and cost three hundred dollars. It was worth every penny.)

ESTATE SALE
Gorgeous Wurlitzer organ w/Leslie spkr, fruitwood dining set w/rush chairs, hutch, tea carts, Brown Jordan furn. Mittereich 412, ironstone, silver, crystal, jewelry, oils, steins, new Schwinn, golf

clubs, tools, fridge, freezer, Waterford cookware, 1st. class kitchen stuff, designer clothes 10-14, handknit sweaters, rest of Imelda's shoes. All best quality. Must sell entire contents. 14424 Wellborn Dr., Huntington Harbour (PCH, turn N. on Chatwin, R. on Channel to Sullivan Island, L. on Payne, Fri & Sat, June 26th & 27th, 8:30-4 P.M.

Give specific driving directions only when you're in an obscure locale, or in a restricted residential area that prohibits sale signs. Never list your phone number in a general ad such as this, as you'll likely be besieged with unwanted calls.

If I'm holding a sale in a retirement community, I run an ad in the weekly paper in addition to my regular weekly ad for my services. A one-day, Thursday ad costs about fifteen to twenty dollars. It can be even more detailed than the one above. I pay for this ad when I place it. I generally don't run an ad in a daily paper for a retirement community sale. (See Holding Sales in a Retirement Community)

The following is a sample ad placed in a retirement community weekly paper. It cost twenty dollars.

Estate Sales

1700 Interlachen 45-B Thursday - Friday, April 16-17, 9-3. Very clean and neat grandmother's household furnishings, chairs, end tables, book case, period dining room set, period floor lamp, silver, bric-a-brac, double and twin beds, (good mattresses), dresser, chests of drawers, linens, sewing machine, Singer, craft items, oodles of small picture frames, good kitchen things, storage cabinets, bird bath, excellent

selection of health books and much more.
Everything nice and tidy and priced to sell.
By (my name)
1458 Alderwood 280-B, 431-0287

When holding a sale in retirement communities such as mine, you are required to give your own address and phone number, as well as the sale address.

Check your area for advertising sources. You may find a free publication such as the Recycler. Don't overlook the local Penny Saver or other weekly publications. Be sure you check rates and deadlines. They vary a great deal. My biggest nightmare is that I'll forget to place an ad or miss a deadline.

Flyers

If I have several sales booked for the upcoming months, I will make up flyers listing them, and will distribute them at my current sale. As well as these flyers, I will have my business cards on the sales table, as I am invariably asked about my services. If you're not too busy, explain your method of working right then. This is one of the best sources of future business as they can see you in action.

Signs

The morning of a sale which will be held in your town or neighborhood, my helper and I set out at around 7 A.M. to place our signs at busy intersections leading to the sale site.

Don't place a sign more than a half mile away if at all possible. Don't attach them to red and white STOP signs (It's illegal in my town.) I may tape them to stop and go signals where I live, however. With any luck, they'll still be in place at the end of the second day. Sale days are usually Friday and Saturday. DO be a good citizen and take the signs down Saturday afternoon. Your signs can be reused. They'll cost over a dollar each to make, and I don't like making them. My daughter hounds me; "Mom, get some better looking signs." "Why?" I ask. "Half of them will be gone when we go to take them down." Your regular customers will come to recognize your familiar sign, and, even if they haven't read your ad, will follow your signs to the sale.

When I first began holding sales, ALL my signs remained in place until Saturday afternoon. Today, I'm lucky to have half left. Here's why:

1. someone wants to use them themself;
2. someone is holding a garage sale and doesn't want competition;
3. the neighbors don't like the looks of them;
4. an annoyed customer who didn't get an item at their price is spiteful.

Those are all the reasons I can think of, but there are probably more. Your signs are very important as they attract all the people who don't see a newspaper; the neighborhood shoppers, and people driving down the streets. A whole lot of people.

Here's how I make mine:

1. poster board. Bright orange. Size eleven by nineteen inches. One large piece will give you two signs nine and a half by eleven inches.
2. two yardsticks from the local lumber year. About forty cents each. I've found these to be the cheapest wood available;
3. wide black marking pen. The kind used for

graffiti;

4.   white poster board. Cut to nineteen by three and a half inches. Try to get six strips from one piece of eleven by nineteen inches. This is for the address and is attached to the bottom. It will be removed after each sale;

5.   stapler, or staple gun. Even small nails;

6.   masking, or electrical tape for attaching signs to sign poles.

MAKE IT BIG AND MAKE IT BOLD. DON'T MAKE IT LOOK TOO GOOD OR IT BECOMES TOO STEALABLE.

Chapter 11

THINGS ELECTRICAL

Electricity and I don't get along.

If an electrical appliance is, or even seems to be faulty, don't sell it even "as-is". Trash it. Do you really need a lawsuit if it blows up at home? The sale of my first electric bed decided me on this course of future action. It worked beautifully at the sale home. Unfortunately, the buyer did not take my advice about hiring reliable movers, and hired a team I remember as "drag and trash" experts. I wasn't too surprised when she called me a day later to tell me about the smoke that was curling from her newly delivered bed after these movers had "dropped" it off. I was surprised, however, when she asked that the entire purchase price be refunded. "It worked perfectly when you bought it" I said. "You tried it out." The fact that the owner of the bed had been paid did nothing to stop the complaints. Two letters later, I decided to refund her the commission I made on the bed and gave her names of electric bed mechanics. My commission would have been enough to pay them.

Electric beds are a big ticket sale, going for one thousand dollars and higher in a retail store. This customer paid a mere hundred and fifty dollars, which included the custom made spread and headboard. I don't like to sell electric beds anymore. For high priced items, an ALL SALES ARE FINAL sign is now backed up by a separate receipt signed by the buyer as to the condition of the merchandise at the time of purchase.

Make sure before each sale all the TVs, stereos, clock radios, and any other electric appliances work. You may be so busy pricing other items that you might forget to test them at all. I recall one sale in which there was a twenty-five inch TV in a lovely cabinet. During the interview, I was told by the client that the TV didn't work. I pushed the ON button - nothing. Trusting me! I marked it "as-is" at fifty dollars. I thought someone would buy it for the cabinet, as people were turning old sets into liquor cabinets at the time.

It didn't sell the first day. On the second, half-price day, in came a different crowd. I call them the "I'll take it off your hands" bargainers. A man went over to this really lovely three-year-old set. "It doesn't work," I said. At that, he picked up the remote which I had taped to the top, and, with a click of a switch, presto - a perfect picture appeared!

It was a TV that apparently had been set up to work

just on the remote. I felt foolish. I'm sure he felt fortunate. "Well, this two hundred dollar set is now yours for twenty-five dollars," I said.

My nine-year-old grandson, who was helping that day, was beside himself. "Grandma, you lost a lot of money," he wailed as we watched the man load it onto his pickup truck. "It's half-price day today," I replied. "It's my fault for not checking it out better." I hoped my client would never find out about the remote. I didn't plan to tell her.

Take no one's word for what works and what doesn't work. Relatives don't know. Or do they? A case in point. A lovely mahogany cabinet housing stereo and record player was said to be in playing condition. I don't know how it could have been, because when I picked up the cord to plug it in to play a record, there was no plug.

Someone had cut the electrical cord in half!

Chapter 12

JEWELRY AND SILVER

Jewelry

Silver and jewelry (antique, costume and even junk) are my favorites sale items. Why? They make a good deal of money for your client and for you; they take up little space, and can be marked, mended and cleaned at home while watching TV.

I mark necklaces, rings and bracelets with small paper tags. I put most earrings on colored index cards. I keep the good jewelry under lock and key. I always ask my clients if I may take the jewelry home to work on.

No one has ever objected.

Don't scoff at junk jewelry. Although most dealers and collectors buy mainly antique and fine jewelry, your every-day customer buys scads of inexpensive costume jewelry. Thirty pairs of earrings at prices of one to five dollars each add up in a hurry. Check and see what the least expensive jewelry is selling for before you begin marking. Most clients have taken the jewelry they want before you begin marking, so any left over after the second day is yours to buy cheaply. Remember, this jewelry can be marketed again and again at other sales, flea markets and swap meets. What doesn't sell in your area may be snapped up at another sale fifteen or twenty miles away. If you want to bring in your own jewelry or other items to a sale, ALWAYS ask for your client's permission. You usually do this if the client has little, or no, jewelry to sell. If you ARE selling some of your own things as well as your clients, be meticulous in record keeping and be sure you keep them separate. I put an "X" on sales tags and index cards of my own jewelry. Careful record keeping, I repeat, is a must. I've seldom kept track of the many hours I've spent marking and tagging. It's a labor of love.

I tell my clients that if I find jewelry that may be valuable, I'll set it aside for them. They can then decide to keep it, or let me sell it. I'll then get other opinions on it's value from dealer friends, other agents or a jeweler.

It's wise to get on a first name basis with a local, reliable jeweler. In exchange for the small price of mending a piece of jewelry (if I can't) or appraising it (usually at no charge), you can send business to him.

Be especially careful in your pricing in this area. You can always lower the price, but it's hard to raise it. You can also decide not to sell the good jewelry at half price the second day. Offer only twenty to twenty-five percent off on that day. A lot of jewelry buyers are avid collectors and don't need a fifty percent inducement.

When you're learning to price jewelry, walk

through jewelry shops, read, study and DON'T HESITATE to ask questions. If you begin getting sales in which there is a lot of good jewelry, invest in a course in gemology. I haven't taken a class yet. I've been able to acquire reliable appraisals by the methods I've already mentioned. Buy and learn to use a jeweler's loupe, and carry it with you. If you haven't mastered it, at the very least it makes you look professional.

This is an area in which you really may encounter "treasure hunting". This is why you must go through a house most carefully, from top to bottom. Examine drawers and clothing, especially pockets, minutely. You may find items behind and under drawers and as far back as possible in closets and on shelves.

I found some very expensive pearls among used makeup at the back of a bathroom drawer. I'd shown them to my clients and they weren't interested in keeping them. "Sell them", they said. I did for fifteen hundred dollars, and they were very pleased.

If a client asks you to be on the lookout for a certain piece of jewelry, do so. Tell them if, or when, you find it. In many cases, though, another relative has found it first, or a deceased has given it away earlier.

Jewelry is the most "stealable" item at a sale, and steal your customer will. I've not only had jewelry stolen, I even had a Chinese lock on my glass topped jewelry case stolen. You must learn to be theft-proof, and you must learn very quickly. To thwart would-be thieves, I finally started to wear the best items; rings with tags on my fingers, pins attached to my sale apron. I'm a walking showcase, but it works. Here are some basic rules:

1.   keep the good jewelry under lock and key, or wear it;

2.   hire an extra sales aide if you have a large amount of jewelry, with the job of showing it and selling it only;
3.   don't put jewelry out the first two hours when you're busiest. If you're working alone, it takes too much time to watch it when crowds are biggest.

Experience and a keen eye will have you pulling Eisenberg, Weiss and Miriam Haskell jewelry out from a heap even before you see the signatures on the back. Signed jewelry brings more than unsigned, and stones held by prongs bring more than glued-in stones.

Silver

Silver, sterling or silver plate, is another area where there's a lot of value in a small amount of merchandise. I find that silver is easier to price, but more difficult to sell, than jewelry.

I've never understood people who discard silver, even silver plate, (only because it needs to be polished), in order to buy stainless flatware. A nice, complete set of boxed silver plate easily sells for $100.00 to $150.00 to a dealer.

Once I was asked by a real estate agent to appraise some antiques for one of her clients. Most of the furniture was to be shipped north, but there was a small antique table I bought for myself. Also left over were two small boxes of odds and ends. I inquired as to what was going to be done with them. "We'll put them on the curb for the trash man," the lady replied. "We've already put out a few boxes and they're gone." I gagged. "I'll buy this box for twenty dollars" I said.

"Great," she answered. She probably would have

given it to me, but I had to pay her something when I spied a silver covered vegetable dish tossed in the bottom of the box. When I got home and polished it, I found it was sterling. It remains one of my favorite pieces.

With time, you'll be able to pick out sterling from silver plate. I used to believe that I could tell sterling from plate by its weight. I thought sterling was lighter, but it's not always so. It must be marked sterling somewhere on the piece, however.

Pricing Sources
Here are some books I have found helpful in identifying and pricing jewelry and silver: (You will eventually have your own favorites).
1.   SILVERPLATED FLATWARE by Tere Hagan. An identification and value guide. It has drawings of patterns.
2.   ART NOUVEAU & ART DECO JEWELRY by Lillian Baker
3.   100 YEARS OF COLLECTIBLE JEWELRY by Lillian Baker
4.   TWENTIETH CENTURY FASHIONABLE PLASTIC JEWELRY by Lillian Baker
All the above are available through Collector Books, P.O. Box 3009, Paducah, KY 42002-3009, 1-800-626-5420.
5.   ENGLISH SILVER HALL-MARKS Edited by Judith Banister.
Published by W. Foulsham & Co., Ltd. 1990
6.   JEWELRY & GEMS, THE BUYING GUIDE by Matlins & Bonanno
Gemstone Press, South Woodstock, VT, 1984.

Chapter 13

THE EYE OF A DEALER

You must develop the eye of a dealer which is a very perceptive eye. Actually, dealers have at least four sets of eyes. They can spot a one sixteenth-inch crack or a minuscule chip at sixteen paces. When I was learning by working alongside another agent (the best way), many times my teacher would pick up a piece I had marked and saw as perfect, only to point out an imperfection.

"You've got to mark this 'as-is'", he said. The fifty dollar Weller bowl now became seven dollar and fifty cent "as-is" item. I am not a dealer. I do not have a mall space, so my house very quickly became filled with "as-is" items. I rescued them just for their beauty. Their value is almost nil. An exception would be old kitchenware which is mostly "as-is" due to use. They are not greatly diminished in value, but a Royal Doulton figurine with a large chip is unsaleable to a dealer.

Dealers need near-perfect merchandise for their retail customers. That's why I can get very good prices for items I sell to them. Remember, dealers need to mark up one hundred percent or double what they pay you in order to cover their rent and operating costs.

Many of my most expensive items will be sold to dealers, who, in turn, will double the price to their customers. Generally, my customers, other than dealers, won't pay fifty dollars for a Shelley cup and saucer. This is especially true when I have sales in a retirement community. Dealers may have antique space in malls in very pricey locales and have an easier time selling higher priced items.

As an estate-sale agent, you cannot afford to hold a Staffordshire figure for the length of time it might take to get top dollar. If you have a dealer customer who buys a certain type of goods, here's where you might make a phone call and sell it.

Remember, you have an entire house to empty in a very short time. This not only includes collectibles, sterling, jewelry, and antiques, but all the other, everyday furnishings. You've got to sell and you've got to sell fast. Dealers are important to you.

After you've marked your collectibles for the sale, you may want to let a few dealers preview, or shop prior to sale days. Have them shop one at a time. Seldom together. They should buy quickly and without any haggling over your price. I had one dealer who kept saying, "I'll give you so much for this" and I stopped allowing her the privilege of previewing. This is strictly a courtesy on your part. You will be up to your eyeballs in organizing the set-up, and the time you spend with a dealer (even though most of them move quickly) takes away from your set-up time. You may spend anywhere from four to one hundred hours to mark a sale.

Another reason I like to allow previews for dealers is that you can test your prices on them. In my area of least expertise, such as tools or Western items, I'll preview to Joe, a very thrifty dealer. If he snaps up some cowboy boots, a poncho or a knife at my price, I know I probably marked them too low. If he passes on them, they may be too high for him to make a profit. But he may also be the only person who is interested in them at any price. He can always make an offer, and you can sell them after the sale. This is a see-saw game.

One dealer taught me a lot about guns, a very specialized area. Now, I don't take anyone's word for value. I found a very fine hunting rifle in a garage at one of my sales. I don't like firearms and was most willing to sell it very cheaply to a dealer who told me that the firing mechanism was jammed, and would cost a great deal to fix. I sold it to him for a song, and later told a friend the make of rifle and the price I got for it. I apparently gave it away. So, when they say, "Oh, the gun is jammed. I'll give you thirty dollars for it," take the time to learn about it. Ask your male relatives to look at it. When you hear the words "I'll take it off your hands", wait. It usually translates to "It's valuable". Don't give it away. Your client expects you to know enough about everything to get top dollar.

Why might you want a dealer's business?
1.   They buy quickly and don't haggle.
2.   You've sold a lot of the priciest goods before the sale, perhaps saving these items from damage or theft.
3.   When you hold the sale, it will be smaller and more manageable. You may need to hire one less person.

4. You've made pre-sale money and have less stress on sale day. It's nice to know going into a sale that you've already sold one thousand dollars worth of goods. Then if it rains on sale day, or if there's a lot of competition with other sales, you've already got money in the bank.

Be fair to dealers and they'll be fair to you.

Chapter 14

DOS AND DON'TS FOR A SALE AGENT

1.   To price, sell and otherwise dispose of a client's goods.

2.   To feed your help on sale days. On sale days, I make and bring a lunch. At a very big sale, I've had it catered. If it's a set-up day, we'll take a break and go out to lunch. Along with shopping the sale on set-up days, this may be your help's only reward. When I set-up alone, I don't go out to lunch. I find it breaks my stride. I am able to work for about 4 to 5 hours straight, but everyone has their own routine. I like to have everything marked and ready a couple of days before a sale, but I know one

agent who can, and seems to enjoy, doing his pricing at the last minute.

3.   To provide security for the sale. If you're having a BIG sale and hiring five or more workers, it's worth hiring a security guard. Your client expects his property to be protected. A professional guard (often an off-duty police officer) charges eighty to one hundred dollars a day. His mere presence, especially if he is in uniform, probably will discourage not only theft, but robbery.

4.   To pay your help from your profits. Usually at least seventy dollars a day. The day may be six to eight hours long. Your best helpers have initiative and won't have to be told to straighten merchandise and tidy up. Some have a natural ability to sell. Others may need to be taught.

5.   To sell an item to a customer even though you wanted to buy it for yourself. You were just too busy to put it aside. The only time it's acceptable to pull out an item is if it happens to be something the client told you about at the last minute, and you neglected to set it aside for them.

This practice doesn't endear you to your customers, but in a pinch: "Gee, I'm sorry. My client called me this morning and asked me to save this." may keep you from losing face.

6.   To not give away your client's merchandise. This seems fairly obvious, but I had two cute spinster sisters in their eighties who came to my sales. After they had spent their allotted amounts (not very much), they'd bring out all kinds of little things, mostly clothes at fifty cents or less, and say something like, "I've spent so much with you. Can't I just have this?" I succumbed to their guile once or twice, but as their spending money decreased, their requests for free goods increased. I finally put a stop to this practice with, "If you had hired me to sell

66

your things, how would you feel if I just gave them away?" They soon took their business to other sales in the area.

7.   If there's an item of furniture or a collectible you want for yourself, have it appraised by a disinterested party. It's hard to be fair to your client if you're also the buyer and appraiser. Be very careful in this area. I don't have a mall space so I don't wear two hats in this respect. I generally err on the side of the client. If I want something badly, I'll pay full price the first day.

8.   To make it fun for your customers and for yourself. I held one sale in which the deceased had Mexican memorabilia galore, down to a matador's cape and original bullfight posters.

I set everything out on serapes, served chips and bean dip and played classical Mexican records.

Chapter 15

DOS AND DONT'S FOR A CLIENT

1.   To let your agent sell the things you said would be for sale.

2.   If you do pull things out after pricing begins, to pay the commission on it, or at least offer to pay.

3.   To arrange (or let me arrange) with real estate agents not to schedule workmen on sale days. One agent on the first day of the sale sent a carpenter and plasterer over to redo the bathroom. I sent them away. She called me in the midst of the very busiest hour of the first day and whined, saying that she didn't know the sale started that day.

     This was the only time they could come and she

wanted to close escrow Monday. She asked me if I "didn't want to see the escrow close quickly?" I allowed them to return later that same morning after we had moved everything from the patio into the house so that they could bring in their equipment. They were still spraying plaster dust everywhere and hammering at four in the afternoon.

Note: Don't expect a lot of cooperation from real-estate agents. Many expect to get first pickings of choice items with the promise of referrals. Only rarely has it worked that way for me. Most of my clients find me through word-of-mouth. The exception to the rule, and there's always at least one, was a nice agent who, although he sat through both sale days as if it were his own open house, provided a well-heeled buyer to pay top dollar for the top-of-line furniture.

And another real estate agent continues to refer me to her clients, although I've yet to meet her.

Chapter 16

DOS AND DONT'S FOR A CUSTOMER

Just like agents and clients, customers also have certain obligations toward making a sale successful. They are:

1. Don't hoard merchandise from other customers just to pick through it later. This is a big NO NO! If you see this happening, stop it as it keeps your most saleable items out of circulation during your best hours - the first two.

2. Don't haggle with my cashier about prices. My cashiers only take money. They don't negotiate price. If you want a better deal, talk to me.

3. Don't remove, or change, price stickers. A remark like "The stickers must have gotten switched. This isn't the correct price!" helps slow down this tendency.

4. Don't steal. Enough said.

5. Don't ask to return a one dollar "as-is" clock that

you know you can fix after you find out you can't.

6.   If a salesperson lowers a price, don't come to the agent or any other salesperson and try to get it lowered further. If you see a customer doing this, stop it and stand by your salesperson. You may even refuse to sell an item to a customer who does this.

7.   Don't put merchandise in a corner or behind things in order to return on half price day and buy it.

8.   Don't spend ten minutes getting a salesperson to lower a price from four dollars to two dollars and fifty cents, (when you wanted it for three dollars) only to present the cashier with a twenty dollar bill.

9.   To have fun.

10.   To provide your own way of moving the couch, barca-lounger or dining-room set you bought.

When I first started, I hauled as much as I could in my car (not a van or truck). Only once did I even get a thank-you. Now, I just say "I'm sorry, I'm not a mover. Here are the names of a few." I keep their names and phone numbers on my sales table. There may be quite a few times when someone lives alone and needs help, but they can usually find a friend or relative to give them a hand if they don't want to pay a mover.

Hold tight to this rule. Just say, "I gave you such a good price for this you can afford to pay to have it moved." Here is a good example of why I've had to take such a stern course about this:

A man, looking very down and out, appeared at one of my sales and said he was sleeping on the floor. He absolutely needed to buy my bed and frame, he said, and must have it delivered that afternoon.

He seemed so pathetic that I enlisted my daughter and her truck, and we delivered it. It had begun to sprinkle as we tugged and hauled the box springs and mattress into his apartment. When we got it in, we found that he already had a bed set up in his bedroom, one that I thought better than the one he had bought from us! He insisted that we drag out the first bed and assemble the new one, all the time complaining about whether it had gotten damp from the rain. This experience was not worth the twenty dollars I had charged him.

You'll be doing enough furniture moving in the course of your sale. You won't need to get into the" professional mover" league.

Chapter 17

YOUR HELP AND YOUR
CUSTOMERS - WARNINGS!

Your Help

Let me tell you about Annie.

I had a very large sale and I needed a lot of sales help. This was a once-in-a-year sale. Great neighborhood, great merchandise. I knew I'd need nine or ten people to work. A friend of mine said she'd worked with this young woman, and she was impressed with her speed and willingness to work. I called Annie a few days before the sale and asked if she could come over one day while I was setting up. I wanted to meet her and explain what I needed her to do. She arrived on time - a bubbly young lady with two cute girls.

The house was completely torn apart and I wondered about the advisability of two small children running loose in it. "Don't worry," she said. "They'll stay in the car." It occurred to me that she might have a baby-sitter problem come sale day. "Oh no," she said. "I have a sitter." She seemed willing and energetic, and I engaged her to work upstairs for the first day of the sale.

Sale day arrived. Annie arrived without her children. I sent her to the second floor and told her I wanted her to monitor the entire upstairs, to help the customers find things and to keep it tidy. There was no money for her to handle. This had been my first job at a sale. It's easy but boring, as you're out of the mainstream. I first realized I had a problem with Annie when she kept drifting downstairs where all the action was. Amidst all the hubbub, I kept shooing her back upstairs. (Remember, you are in charge and must keep an eye on EVERYTHING.) Once or twice, I had to break up a tete-a-tete with Annie and one of my other sales people when I found them hanging out in the backyard during a busy period. I finally heard Annie arranging with the wrapper to switch jobs. I said no. They had worked it out between themselves until I called a halt. I wanted my wrapper to learn the job as she was also new to the game. If anyone was going to do any switching, it was going to be me.

Annie had this enormous amount of energy. I had a driveway just crammed with boxes of garage tools which I needed moved to the other side to make way for a truck. "I'll move it," she said, and immediately leaped in and started throwing boxes around. I was still trying to corral her back upstairs. "What's with Annie?" I asked Bill, my clean-up and garage man. Man-of-the-world, he replied, "Oh, she's high on speed."

Speed I like, but not drug induced. Bill and I dubbed her "Amphetamine Annie"!

Annie wanted to come back at the end of the sale

to clean up for me. I was not going to be there, so I said "No, the house will be locked, and I can't come by." "Oh, I know how to get in," she replied. Gee, she'd been a busy bee. And when I saw her making frequent phone calls during the sale, I asked her if there was a problem. "No," she answered. "I'm just checking on my kids. The baby sitter didn't show up." Had she even hired one?

I paid her and fervently hoped we'd never cross paths again. I could only imagine the chaos she'd create if she had succeeded in switching jobs and had gotten to the wrapping table or the cash register. She certainly hadn't done much tidying upstairs, although she was a whiz at hauling "nuts and bolts".

Everyone, it seems, will want to work for you. Be very selective about who you use. Try hiring on a trial basis. You'll find out in a hurry if they have what you need - agility of body and mind, a rapport with the customers and your other help, honesty, and, most importantly, the willingness to find out what needs to be done and to do it.

Your Customers

Don't jump to conclusions about customers based on their attire. I recall one very large sale I held, that included a great deal of fine antiques, including Bergere and Bedemeir chairs and Royal Dux porcelain. One very seedy looking couple came in early on the first day. The woman had on an old cotton housedress and run-down shoes, and the man wore blue work pants and a soiled shirt.

They expressed interest in several pieces of the best antique furniture. I didn't pay much attention to them as I was extremely busy, until the man approached me and said they wanted to buy the chairs. I was dubious of their solvency but what can you say to someone with greasy hands when they sit down and write you a check for twelve hundred dollars? They said they would return later that day (a Friday) to pick up the furniture. I felt I needed to check out their check by calling the bank, but there was no working phone at the sale house. I was quite nervous about the liquidity of the Joneses, enough so that as soon as I closed for the day, I leaped into my car and drove the fifteen miles to their bank with their check in my hand. I cashed it on the spot. The teller seemed friendly so I ventured a question about the Joneses. "What kind of business does Mr. Jones have?" I inquired. I'd been too busy to find this out at the sale. "Oh, he's a very good customer," replied the teller. "He owns his own tool and die business."

We became very well acquainted over the next months as they became quite active customers. They liked to tell me of their fine collection of antique carpets and furniture. I often visualize them showering and changing into Victorian clothing to pour a glass of claret from a Baccarat decanter while they perch on the Bedemeir side chairs to discuss nuts and bolts.

A word to the wise: reserve judgment of a client's financial status. Don't base it on dress alone, like I foolishly did. Customers often dress down, hoping to get the best bargains. You can also learn a lot about people by taking the time to chat with them as they shop.

Chapter 18

FINDING SALES IN ODD PLACES

Be flexible as to where and how you hold a sale. I have never bought an entire house full of furniture, as some agents do. I've been told this is a possibility and I have, on infrequent occasions, been asked to purchase all the furnishings in a house.

Either my price was too low, or I talked myself out of it, usually by saying something to a client like, "You can really make more money if I hold a sale for you than if I buy it all."

I did, however, buy about half the contents of a storage locker. The storage fees after a year were becoming prohibitive. The client was a friend of a friend so I went out to see it. The goods were stored in a multilevel storage building where it would have been impossible to hold a sale. (This is something to consider when a family member dies, and you're debating selling, or storing.) I went back twice and purchased some small items plus four tables and three dressers. They were all collectibles and I carted them home in my car and a truck. I turned my home into a shop, setting everything on the tables and dressers. I called in dealers one at a time, and sold about three-fourths of the goods. I knew I could sell the rest at flea markets. It was a huge success and I doubled my money. Be aware, though, of your available space. The little things were easy to sell, but the big things (the dressers) seemed to get bigger, especially the one blocking my hallway.

I'd think twice about doing it again. It was an enormous amount of work, but I made money and helped my client solve her storage problem.

Chapter 19

WORKING ALONE

If you're a "fraidycat", this isn't a business for you. If I'm working inside a retirement community, I feel very safe setting up alone and holding the sale alone. But outside of a retirement community, I take certain precautions. I may set up alone, but after the "pulpit incident", I don't hold a sale by myself.

It happened like this:

I was holding a sale in a pleasant, middle-class neighborhood and foresaw no problems working alone. About two hours into the first day when the sales rush was over, a woman came in and introduced herself.

"I'm Leah," she said.

When I showed no reaction, she asked, "Didn't they tell you I'd be here today?"

"No", I replied. I never had heard her name mentioned. She rushed from room to room, apparently searching for something.

"Did you put aside the table and lace cloth for me?" she demanded.

"No", I replied.

I'm sure my face was as blank as my mind. Who was she? She went on to describe the mahogany lamp table to me, and I realized it was part of the set I had sold an hour before.

"You're too late. I sold it."

"You were supposed to have put it aside", she yelled at me. She came unglued and screamed,

"You're a liar. Do you know what that was?"

"I hadn't a clue. It looked like a lamp table to me. She kept getting more excited by the minute.

"I was Mrs. Browns housekeeper. She was a minister. We had weekly prayer meetings here and it was our pulpit."

I repeated that no one had told me about its true purpose, and she told me I was lying and to "Go to hell". At this point, I told her to leave. I was still trying to keep things under control.

"Does your religion teach you to curse people?" I asked. This only added fuel to her fire. Her face reddened.

"No one tells me to leave", and she damned me again.

There was no useable phone in the house, and I honestly thought that she was about to strike me when a man and woman came in. She backed down when she saw the man and left in a furious rage. I now understood one of the reasons I was engaged for the sale. The clients didn't want to deal with her. Since the "pulpit incident", I no longer work alone.

When I begin a sale, one of the first things I do is to knock on the neighbors' doors on either side of the house. I introduce myself and give them my card. This is for two reasons. They may have a Neighborhood Watch program and wonder who's rummaging around next door, and you may need to call on them in case of an emergency, such as the one I just recounted. My main purpose, however, is to establish a rapport in the neighborhood. You're doing this one sale, but if you do a good job, you may get more sales on the block. Word-of-mouth is your very best form of advertising. In several cases, I've done two and three sales for the same family.

I often invite the next-door neighbor in after I've set up, and let them look around and buy something, if they are so inclined. Good will is very important. The neighbors will be giving up their parking spaces the two days of the sale and the week or so before when you and your helpers and dealers will be in and out.

I lock myself in a house. In a very large home, I usually check the premises each morning. I had a sale in a two-story, four-bedroom, three-bath home in a lovely, older residential area that was beginning to get a "tough" reputation.

I don't have a dog, or I'd take it with me. If the next-door neighbors do, I ask them to introduce me to the family pet. When I pull into the driveway each day, I call the dog's name, and let it get to know my voice. It may be the only living thing you talk to all day.

At one sale site, the glass in the back door was broken. I suggested it be fixed. It never was. I covered it with electrical tape. Your safety may not be paramount in your client's mind, but it should be in yours.

One sale in particular comes to mind when I think about working alone. I was still recovering from the "pulpit incident." One morning while setting up, I received a call from a grandson of the owner who had moved to a retirement home a few months before. The young man and I had a nice chat. He asked for his grandmother, and I introduced myself and told him why I was there and the grandmother wasn't. Coincidentally, I had come across an unsealed Christmas card that morning addressed to him that had a fifty dollar bill inside. I told him I would give it to his mother for him. He asked where his grandmother was living, but I didn't have her address (the daughters were the executors). I suggested he contact his mother, and I gave him her number which he didn't have . I thought that was odd.

That evening, I called his mother and told her about the call from the son. A long silence followed. When she finally replied, she sounded stunned. No one had seen or heard from him for the past two years since he'd been released from a lock-up psychiatric facility.

Apparently, he'd surfaced to borrow money from his grandmother. Perhaps he'd driven by or even gotten in (I was later told he knew several means of gaining access). Seeing no grandmother in residence, and her bedroom furniture gone, he'd chanced a phone call. He never contacted his mother.

I was told never to let him in if he came to the door. How was I supposed to keep him out, I wondered? As far as I could determine, he never got in or else he would probably have found grandma's police pistol and rifle which we didn't find until just before the sale.

Yes, they were loaded.

The moral of this story, if there is one, is that no one is going to tell you about any relatives who may be a problem, even though you may ask.

PLAY IT SAFE!

Chapter 20

HOLDING SALES IN A
RETIREMENT COMMUNITY

What's good about it?

1.   If you live in one, you can go home for lunch, or do the laundry while working.
2.   Almost all the residences have the same layout and are about the same size, square footage-wise.
3.   You can usually hold a sale by yourself or with just one other helper.
4.   Safety. A gated community screens non-residents.
5.   Sales are generally smaller and take less time to set up. Your work hours also are shorter. The rules set by my association limit me to between 9 A.M. and 3 P.M. At first, I didn't like this, but I've come to enjoy these "bankers' hours".

6.   A lot of domestics working in retirement communities need furniture and buy a lot of goods for themselves
and to send overseas. These people include care- givers,
housekeepers, maintenance people, roofers and
gardeners.

I enjoy the roofers. They often send a foreman in
near the end of the second day to spot things and to
introduce himself. He will be the one that speaks the
best English. If he feels welcome, he'll bring back the
"guys" to shop. This is a good time for you to sell that
large overstuffed chair or sofa. Many of the roofers
desperately need affordable things, and if you really like
to "wheel and deal", it can be fun. You've probably
already boxed up a lot of things that didn't sell, and I've
often been able to sell a whole box to them. Remember,
"one man's junk is another man's treasure." These are
the people who make it fun and easy.

On the other hand, you may have difficulty
training people in your method of selling, and train them
you must. These are the intense bargainers, and if your
sense of humor is down or your blood pressure up, you
may have a problem.

Be very firm, and don't budge on your price once
you've named it or they will pin you down and argue.
When you've mastered these customers, (I say my price
and turn my back), you'll be able to shop or not shop
anywhere in the world.

What's bad about it?

1.   You must have a permission slip signed by a
director of the retirement community. This is a
Permission-to-Hold-a-Sale document, stating the
conditions of a sale; namely the hours and location, and
that you will not add anything from another sale or
anything of your own to the sale. If you do add goods to
a sale, you can be barred from holding a sale in my

retirement community for a year. You must have this signed to give to the community newspaper before you can run your ad. As this is the only ad you'll need, you can see its effectiveness. This document also controls the next bad thing about retirement community sales:

2.   It's hard to get non-residents inside the gate. Security discourages outsiders and just plain makes it a "pain in the neck" to get them in. Many customers who come to my outside sales would come to these too, but just don't want the hassle.

In some cases, I give my own name and pretend they're friends coming to visit me. An example. I ran an ad in an outside newspaper for a large sale inside the community. I received a least thirty calls from people wanting to attend. I wrote down all the names on a list and left it at the security office as instructed. I never saw any of the people. They either didn't get in or went to another sale once inside. I've pretty much come to the conclusion that it is not worth the hassle to me to bring in outsiders. This is why I began previewing sales.

3.   You're not allowed to post signs on the streets.

4.   Most retirement community residents have all the large furniture they can use. This is another reason to preview to outsiders. Retirees buy mostly small items.

5.   People living inside the retirement community won't pay the prices I can get outside. I price twenty-five percent lower inside the gate. Retiree shoppers buying at sales inside a gated community live in a shopper's paradise.

Chapter 21

TOOLS OF THE TRADE

Here is a list of material you'll need to set up, work and complete an estate sale:

Cleaning supplies for set-up

CARD TABLES. I own over twenty. I use about ten to twelve per sale, but sometimes you may have to set up one sale before you have finished another. When you're buying card tables from sales, try to buy only the lightweights. If you have to keep them in an overhead storage locker as I do, you'll appreciate the light ones.

You also may want one or two longer, folding, picnic-type tables for your cashiers. Unless you have a van or truck, however, you may find these too big to get inside the trunk of your car.

Obviously, the more tables you bring to a sale, the more you have to bring home. You always can use furniture tops, counters and dresser tops to display merchandise.

FOLDING CHAIRS for your cashiers. SCREWDRIVERS and other small tools to take apart furniture, especially beds. LUGGAGE to carry your supplies. A PORTABLE RACK for a sale with lots of clothing. These can be rented. I turned one attached garage into a boutique at one sale.

TABLE CLOTHS to cover your card tables. A twin bed, wash-and-wear sheet will cover three tables and hang down just enough to cover your empty supply boxes stored underneath. LACE TABLE CLOTHS to show off your finest collectibles. SIGNS to post "KEEP OUT", "ALL SALES FINAL", "NO SMOKING" etc. Lots of clean, used PLASTIC GROCERY BAGS, and NEWSPAPERS to wrap china and bric-a-brac. Don't forget cleanser, dish soap and bug spray.

Record Keeping

CALCULATORS with tapes, your BUSINESS CARDS, RULER, FLYERS of any future sales, RECEIPT BOOK, five-by-eight inch, yellow lined SCRATCH PADS to write items sold and amount received.

Eight-and-a-half-by-eleven inch, yellow LINED PADS to transfer scratch pad information, your LETTERHEAD on which to do the final tally.

Pricing

Avery's color coded LABELS, one thousand to a box, three-quarter inch round or any similar sticker. Buy several colors. Several small STAPLERS, a STAPLE GUN for sign making, GREASE PENCILS, BROAD BLACK MARKING PENS for big signs. You may have to ask the sales clerk for the large size as they're not always on the counter. FINE MARKING PENS for pricing your sales stickers. Write as big and as dark as possible for clarity. CLEAR PLASTIC TAPE to put signs on walls - be careful with tape on painted surfaces as tape can remove paint. MASKING TAPE to bundle sets of towels and sheets. ELECTRICAL TAPE is good for attaching signs to posts with, although it's more expensive than masking tape. Be careful about using cheap tape. Many cheap brands won't hold for two days outdoors on a post. That's why I use electrical tape if I have it.

Selling

Exchange your old work apron for a neat, clean SALE-DAY APRON. I had some made from lightweight, wash-and-wear, ticking with one small pocket at the top and a generous pocket all across the bottom.

This not only keeps your sales staff clean, but it makes it possible for your customers to identify the sellers from the buyers. EXTRA LABELS, and a STAPLER, PENS and NOTE PADS for your pockets, and you're ready.

Chapter 22

SO YOU STILL WANT TO
BE AN ESTATE SALES AGENT?

You've read the book. Your aunt just died and you're her executor, and you're ready to tackle the job at hand. Stop right here and hire an estate-sales agent if you're only interested in making enough from the sale for that new twenty-four foot sailboat you've got your eye on. "No," you say. "I want to do it myself." So what if the big old house is fifteen miles from your home and you have a full time job. You've got a wife and grown children. They'll be glad to help you. Or will they? Luckily, they are, and it only costs you lunches and three-quarters of the family antiques. You still end up with a little extra money and a strong urge to do it again. You've been bitten.

Benefits of holding sales

1.   You'll be the first in line (after the heirs) to buy that Roseville bowl or the lovely piece of old sandwich glass.

2.   You'll have a chance to earn extra dollars. If you keep careful records, you'll find the money you earn can vary from twenty-five cents an hour to as much as fifteen dollars. An example is collecting on a bad check. Even though your cashier got a driver's I.D. number and a work phone number, it's been returned to you (remember it's made out to you) and you've had absolutely no luck in collecting it. You're now out two hundred and fifty dollars for a Victorian table. You can hardly go to your client and ask for a rebate. After all, that is one of the reasons he hired you in the first place; so that he can relax. You finally turn the check over to the police and receive a receipt from them. You hope they can succeed where you failed, and they very often can. Be reminded at this point that once you give them the check, you give up your right to any further pursuit of your "customer". Incidents such as this can whittle away at your earning power very quickly.

3.   This job will get you and keep you in shape. However, I recommend a jacuzzi for those strained muscles after you've spent a day on the job.

4.   It's fun. Treasure hunting should be.

5.   It teaches you about human nature. The good as well as the bad.

6.   It provides a service. I altruistically considered this my primary reason for embarking on this career. A surly gatekeeper in a restricted neighborhood challenged my remark about helping people with his own, saying that "the only person I was helping was myself". After holding "umpteen" sales, I've decided that we were both correct. It helps others as well as yourself.

7.   Leads to other jobs. Your work and experience and knowledge will open lots of doors for you. The possibilities are unlimited. You can hold your own sales after learning how from this book. You can be paid for working for another agent at their sales, or become a dealer and open your own mall space using the collectibles you've gathered. You can also work on a regular basis or infrequent basis for yourself or others at flea markets or swap meets.

Reminders
1.   Your VERY best advertising is word of mouth. One happy client with a check in hand, an empty house ready to list for sale and a receipt from a charitable organization on their desk is better than the most expensive ad you can run in any publication. A recommendation to the client's friends will expand like ripples made by a pebble thrown into a pond. You won't have to worry about where to find clients; you'll only need to save some time for yourself.
2.   A good sale agent, one who knows how to price, appraise, organize and sell, can make more money for a client even after the agent pays themself a commission, than a client can earn for themself without paying any commission to an agent.
3.   Be selective in what you buy for yourself. Keep your own collections small, thimbles or pens or money, or before long, you'll be forced to build onto your own home, or move into that big old house of your aunt's to open an antique business.

Summing up
     I hope this book will have helped you bypass the land mines and enabled you to locate your personal gold

mines - whether they are added income, additions to your own personal collections, the satisfaction of the service you've done for others, or maybe the most important benefit will be an ever-increasing awareness of your entrepreneurial abilities.

Whatever the reasons, I wish you success.

INDEX

NOTES

NOTES

NOTES

NOTES

NOTES

HAVE SALE - WILL TRAVEL

$ecrets of an Estate-$ale Agent

★ A Users Guide To The Perfect Estate Sale ★

Order Your Copy Now

- -

Rising Eagle Publishers
P.O. Box 3813
Seal Beach, CA 90740-7813

*Launching Into
The 21ˢᵗ Century*

Please send _____ copies of HAVE SALE - WILL TRAVEL to:

Name _____

Company _____

Address _____

City _____ State _____ Zip _____

Enclose check or money order for $14.95 for each book, plus $2.00 shipping and handling; $1.50 for each additional copy.

Please add $1.15 sales tax to orders shipped to California addresses.

Canada - $16.95 plus $2.00 shipping.

Make checks payable to Rising Eagle Publishers